50 Quick and Easy Lesson Activities

By Mike Gershon

About the Author

Mike Gershon is a teacher, trainer and writer. He is the author of twenty books on teaching, learning and education, including a number of bestsellers, as well as the co-author of one other. Mike's online resources have been viewed and downloaded more than 2.5 million times by teachers in over 180 countries and territories. He is a regular contributor to the Times Educational Supplement and has created a series of electronic CPD guides for TES PRO. Find out more, get in touch and download free resources at www.mikegershon.com

Training and Consultancy

Mike is an expert trainer whose sessions have received acclaim from teachers across England. Recent bookings include:

- *Improving Literacy Levels in Every Classroom*, St Leonard's Academy, Sussex

- *Growth Mindsets, Effective Marking and Feedback* Ash Manor School, Aldershot

- *Effective Differentiation,* Tri-Borough Alternative Provision (TBAP), London

Mike also works as a consultant, advising on teaching and learning and creating bespoke materials for schools. Recent work includes:

- *Developing and Facilitating Independent Learning,* Chipping Norton School, Oxfordshire

- *Differentiation In-Service Training,* Charles Darwin School, Kent

If you would like speak to Mike about the services he can offer your school, please get in touch by email: mike@mikegershon.com

Other Works from the Same Authors

Available to buy now on Amazon:

How to use Differentiation in the Classroom: The Complete Guide

How to use Assessment for Learning in the Classroom: The Complete Guide

How to use Questioning in the Classroom: The Complete Guide

How to use Discussion in the Classroom: The Complete Guide

How to Teach EAL Students in the Classroom: The Complete Guide

More Secondary Starters and Plenaries

Secondary Starters and Plenaries: History

Teach Now! History: Becoming a Great History Teacher

The Growth Mindset Pocketbook (with Professor Barry Hymer)

How to be Outstanding in the Classroom

Also available to buy now on Amazon, the entire 'Quick 50' Series:

About the Series

The 'Quick 50' series was born out of a desire to provide teachers with practical, tried and tested ideas, activities, strategies and techniques which would help them to teach brilliant lessons, raise achievement and engage and inspire their students.

Every title in the series distils great teaching wisdom into fifty bite-sized chunks. These are easy to digest and easy to apply – perfect for the busy teacher who wants to develop their practice and support their students.

Acknowledgements

As ever I must thank all the fantastic colleagues and students I have worked with over the years, first while training at the Institute of Education, Central Foundation Girls' School and Nower Hill High School and subsequently while working at Pimlico Academy and King Edward VI School in Bury St Edmunds.

Thanks also to Alison and Andrew Metcalfe for a great place to write and finally to Gordon at KallKwik for help with the covers.

Table of Contents

Newspaper Front-Page

Formal Debate

Pros and Cons

Speech Writing

Peer-Assessment

Self-Assessment

Investigations

Case Studies

Creative Writing

Learning Reviews

Review Writing

Teacher Quizzes

Student Quizzes

Exam Questions

Compare and Contrast

Flow-Charts

Spider Diagram

Glossaries

Comprehension

Keyword Practice

Guides, Leaflets and Posters

Continuum

Student Teachers

Introduction

Welcome to '50 Quick and Easy Lesson Activities.'

This book is all about the activities you use in lessons. We all know how time-consuming planning can be, especially when we have so much else to do on a day-to-day basis.

Here you will find 50 fantastic activities clearly explained, ready for you to pick up and put into practice. Each one is appropriate for use across the curriculum and with different age groups.

Maybe you want a great discussion activity or an effective group work task? Perhaps a way to develop literacy skills or a task which will help students think critically?

Whatever you are after, this book holds the key to planning fantastic, creative lessons which allow pupils to make great progress.

So read on and enjoy! And don't forget, the activities are not set in stone – you can adapt them to suit your teaching style as well as the needs of the particular students you teach.

Speed Debating

01 Speed debating is like shopping on Christmas Eve – fast, frenetic and in need of your complete attention. The only difference is that speed debating is really rather enjoyable.

Introduce your class to a statement such as: 'This house believes democracy is the best of all governments.'

Divide the class in two and explain that one half will be 'for' the statement and one half will be 'against.' Give students 10 minutes to develop their arguments in groups.

When the time is up, ask your students to get into pairs. Every pair should have a 'for' student and an 'against' one. 'For' students get to speak first. They put forward their arguments for one minute as their partner listens. The roles then swap over. Finally, there are 45 seconds during which both students can argue at the same time.

Once that time is up, ask one half of each pair to stand up and find a new partner. The activity then repeats, making speed debating a little bit like speed dating!

Silent Debate

02 Take five large sheets of paper. On each one, write a question or statement connected to the topic. Ideally, these should be fairly (or very) contentious.

Distribute the sheets around the room.

Ask pupils to take a pen and stand up. They must walk around the room and visit each sheet in turn. They should read the questions/statements and then write on their own views, using their pen. When students have commented on all five sheets, they should go back and start commenting on other people's comments.

Throughout the activity, students should remain silent. Any who speak can be sent to the 'naughty corner' for 30 seconds!

Card Talk

03 Create a pack of eight cards. Each card should have a question on it connected to the topic you are studying.

Divide the class into groups of four. Give each group a pack of cards and ask them to appoint a leader and a scribe. The leader will lead the discussion and the scribe will make notes about what is said (although, of course, they can still take part in the debate).

Indicate that groups should select their first card at random from the pack and then begin discussing the question on it. After 3 or 4 minutes have passed, ask groups to pick a second card at random. Repeat this 3 or 4 times overall for the best result.

As you might have guessed, the activity works well when all the questions connect to one another.

Question Porters

04 Divide the class into seven groups. Ask each group to nominate a porter. These students come to the front of the room.

You should give each porter a piece of paper and a question connected to the topic. Each porter should receive a different question.

Porters return to their groups and share their questions. The students discuss these while the porters make notes.

After 4-5 minutes, ask porters to stand up and move to the next group, taking their questions and notes with them. Here, they should outline what has already been discussed and then facilitate a further discussion with their new group.

Repeat the process 3-4 times for the best results.

Goldfish Bowl

05 Divide the class in two. One half arranges themselves in a circle in the middle of the room. The second half arrange themselves around the outside of the circle.

You should sit with the students in the circle.

Introduce a discussion topic and facilitate a discussion with the pupils in the circle. While this is happening, students on the outside make notes, identifying good comments, examples of excellent speaking and listening, and arguments or ideas which they believe have been missed.

The teacher stops the discussion at specific points and asks the pupils on the outside to share their observations and analyses. Hence, it is as if the inner circle are in a goldfish bowl being scrutinised by their peers.

Listening Triads

06 Divide the class into groups of three. Present a topic for discussion. You could give a single statement or question, a series of questions or a series of areas about which you would like pupils to discuss.

In each group, students should decide who will be the observer and who will be the discussers.

When this has been settled, discussers talk about whatever has been presented while the observer listens and makes notes. You might like to give specific instructions regarding what to make notes on.

After 3-4 minutes have passed, signal for discussions to stop. The observer now shares their feedback with their peers.

Repeat a further two times (with the same or different topics) so that all pupils have a chance to take on each role.

Jigsawing

07 Divide the class into groups of five. Display five different tasks on the board connected to the topic, numbered 1-5. Ask students to number themselves 1-5 in their groups. The numbers equate to the tasks.

Groups now break up.

New groups form based on the tasks. So, all the students who are number ones get together, all the number twos get together and so on.

Pupils work on their tasks in their new groups.

After sufficient time has passed, request that the original groups re-form. Here, students take it in turns to teach each other what they have learnt during the course of the activity.

Envoys

08 Divide the class into groups of four. Give each group a different task to complete, a different area of the topic to research or a different question to answer. Indicate how long groups have to complete their work and to become experts in whatever you have given them to do.

When the time is up, ask each group to select an envoy. This person stands up and takes their notes with them to the next group, whereupon they teach their peers what they have been learning about.

Repeat the process until each envoy has visited each group and everyone in the class has had a chance to learn about all the different topics.

Marketplace

09 Divide the class into groups of four. Give each group a different topic to research and set a time limit within which the research needs to be completed.

When the time is up, ask groups to set their tables up like a market stall. They should make a sign indicating what it is they have been researching.

Half of each group remain at their stalls while half leave to visit other stalls.

Students 'sell' their information to each other, swapping what they have learnt until such a time as when all pupils have found out about all the research areas.

You might like to provide students with sheets on which to make notes about each topic.

Interviewing

10 Introduce the topic of study and explain that pupils will be interviewing each other to find out what their peers know, what their opinions are or what experiences they have of the matter in question.

Students work in pairs to come up with between 6 and 10 questions to use for their interviews (the exact number will depend on how much time you have available). You might want to provide some examples to help guide them.

When this has been done, pupils set off and interview their peers. Set a target for the number of interviews you want students to complete.

Conclude the activity with a discussion or by having pupils write up their findings (or both).

Student Presentations

11 Divide the class into groups of four and give each group a different question, topic or area of study to research. Explain that groups will need to create a presentation for their particular issue. Provide students with a set of success criteria. This is particularly important as it will help pupils to appreciate exactly what it is you want them to do with their presentations.

Give an appropriate amount of time for the activity. This will depend on the class you are working with and what it is they are making their presentations about.

When the time is up two options are open to you.

First, you can ask each group to present to the class in turn.

Second, you can ask groups to pair up and to take it in turns to present to each other.

Hot-Seating

12 Invite one student to come to the front of the class and take the hot-seat! They must answer questions from the rest of the class about the topic of study. If appropriate, they can do this in character (for example, if the topic of study is World War Two they could answer questions in the character of Winston Churchill).

When the first pupil has had their turn, invite a second one up and change the topic or the character.

As an alternative, divide the class into groups of four and ask one person in each group to enter the 'hot-seat' while their peers bombard them with questions (before swapping over as outlined above).

Role-Play

13 Role-play can work in many different ways. Here are just three examples:

Divide the class into pairs. Present two characters connected to the topic and ask pairs to devise and then role-play a conversation between these two people.

Divide the class into groups of four. Present a scenario or group of characters and ask students to create a role-play connected to these which illustrates important ideas or keywords connected to the topic.

Divide the class into groups of three. Ask each group to prepare a role-play in which they show the learning being used in a real-world context. Groups then take it in turns to show their work to one another.

Shopping Channel

14 Divide the class into groups of three. Explain that each group needs to create a feature for a shopping channel 'selling' the benefits of knowing about the topic of study (or an aspect of it). Provide a set of success criteria which students can use to structure their work. For example:

- Tell the audience what key information they need to know about the topic.

- Explain why the topic is important and how it relates to other things.

- Use persuasive language to convince the audience that they should 'buy into' this learning.

Finish the activity by having groups show their pieces of work to one another.

Freeze-Frame

15 Divide the class into groups of four. Introduce a statement or scenario connected to the topic of study. Ask students to work in their groups to create a freeze-frame which somehow links to or represents the statement or scenario.

A freeze-frame is a dramatic moment in which the action has been stopped – as if someone has just pressed pause on the DVD player.

Students have to think about what their freeze-frame will focus on, as well as what happened before and what would happen after the point at which they have frozen the action.

Finish the activity by having pupils show their freeze-frames to one another (you may want to have half the class showing at a time, with the other half walking around observing).

Design Brief

16 Students can do this activity individually, in pairs or in groups. It works as follows:

Present the class with a design brief akin to what a design company might receive from a client. The brief should be made up of two things:

- The task you want students to do.

- A set of success criteria you want pupils to fulfil when doing the task.

Indicate that, beyond this, it is up to students to decide how they will tackle the activity.

With this simple approach you are able to present your pupils with a great opportunity to be highly creative as well as a chance to work independently.

Comic Strip

17 Ask students to work individually to create a comic strip visualising something connected to their learning. You can find free templates at http://donnayoung.org/art/comics.htm.

Examples of what the comic strips might be about include:

- An event

- A process

- An interaction between groups or individuals

- An idea

- Hypothetical possibilities

Alternatives

18 Ask your students to come up with a set of alternatives for a given topic, scenario or question. They could do this individually, in pairs or in groups. Here are five example tasks and questions:

Come up with three alternative readings of Robert Frost's poem 'The Road not Taken'.

Develop two alternative methods for investigating whether air pressure is different depending on one's altitude.

Sketch out and then test three alternative methods for measuring curved spaces.

Suggest three alternative conclusions we might draw from these sources. Discuss your ideas with a partner.

What alternatives might there be to increased building in the inner-city?

Advertising

19 Advertising involves many different things. Two of the most important are knowing what you are selling inside out and understanding how to persuade prospective customers that they should buy your product.

This makes advertising a great basis for lesson activities!

Ask your students to create advertising campaigns for ideas or information they have studied. This will see them analysing those things in detail to make sure they know them inside out and then thinking critically about how to present what they know in a persuasive manner.

What If...?

20 Ask students 'What if...?' questions to get them thinking creatively.

You could use one of these questions to start a discussion, to underpin an independent writing task, or to facilitate a creative, design-focussed activity.

And why not encourage your students to come up with their own 'What if...?' questions connected to the topic? They could then follow these through, exploring the ideas to see where they lead.

For a large selection of ready-made 'What if...?' questions, have a look at my free resource 'The What If...? Box' available at www.mikegershon.com/resources/.

Newspaper Front-Page

21 Divide the class into groups of three. Set students the task of creating a newspaper front-page reporting on the topic of study (or a particular aspect of it). You can find free templates at https://www.tes.co.uk/teaching-resource/Newspaper-template-3003960/.

You might like to increase the challenge on this task by giving pupils the topic and then leaving it up to them to do all the research and to work out how best to present this in a newspaper format.

Alternatively, you can give students greater direction by providing the exact information they need to research as well as some suggestion as to how they might best present this.

Formal Debate

22 Introduce students to a proposition connected to the topic of study. For example: 'This house believes that war should not be waged for economic reasons.'

Divide the class in two and explain that half the class will be arguing in favour of the proposition while the other half argue against.

Give students 15-20 minutes to work together to develop their arguments. Each side should pick out three people who will speak on their behalf (a proposer, a seconder and a closer). Students who are not going to speak should come up with questions they can ask the opposing team.

When the time is up, invite the speakers to the front and lead a formal debate, giving time for questions towards the end.

If you have not conducted a formal debate before, you can find advice at www.debatingmatters.com.

Pros and Cons

23 A very simple activity this one, but always useful for helping students to evaluate and assess the information and ideas they are learning about.

Whatever it is you are teaching, ask pupils to identify the pros and cons, the strengths and weaknesses or the benefits and limitations of some or all of the things in question. For example, you might ask them to look at the pros and cons of:

- Arguments

- Ideas

- Changes

- Various alternatives

- Actions

You can extend the activity by asking students to rank the pros and cons they come up with from most to least important (and then to explain why they have made these choices).

Speech Writing

24 Students work individually or in pairs to write a speech advocating for a given position. Examples include:

- Write a speech explaining why you think economic intervention is better than economic regulation.

- Write a speech defending your interpretation of Whitman's poem.

- Write a speech explaining why we should build a bigger playground at the school.

- Write a speech outlining the reasons why we should elect you as class representative.

- Write a speech advocating for a change in the law on littering.

Peer-Assessment

25 Peer-assessment helps students in many ways. First, it gives them a chance to compare their own work to that of their peers. This helps them to develop a greater sense of what can be done. Second, it opens up success criteria, ensuring pupils can become more familiar with what they need to do to succeed. Third, it allows students to think of new ideas based on what they see while engaged in the task.

You can ask pupils to peer-assess any work produced in class or at home. Just make sure they have a mark scheme or set of criteria to use and that you train them on how to give good feedback (that is clear and focussed on the learning).

Self-Assessment

26 Self-assessment brings some of the same benefits as peer-assessment. Again, you can ask pupils to self-assess any work they produce in class or at home. Here are three methods you might employ:

- Ask students to identify three things they have done well and one thing they could do to improve.

- Ask pupils to assess whether or not they have effectively applied their most recent target and then to explain why this was the case.

- Challenge students to identify one piece of their work they could improve and then to improve it there and then.

Investigations

27 Set up an investigation which students have to complete in groups of two or three. What you want them to investigate will depend on what you are teaching but, regardless, the activity will encourage pupils to think critically, to analyse information carefully and to be independent.

You should provide students with the necessary research materials as well as a structure they can use to underpin their investigations (for example, a series of questions they can attempt to answer one-by-one).

At the end of the activity, pupils can write up the whole investigation or just focus on summarising the results of their work.

Case Studies

28 Case studies are a brilliant way to contextualise abstract information. They situate abstract ideas in the real-world, thus making it easier for pupils to understand and assimilate these. In short, case studies are examples writ large.

Ask students to work in pairs. Give each pair a case-study or two connected to the topic along with a set of questions they should use to analyse the material.

After sufficient time has passed, invite pairs to get together in fours in order to share and compare their answers.

Creative Writing

29 You need not confine creative writing to English lessons. It can be used right across the curriculum. Creative writing includes stories, scenes from a play, monologues, imaginary interviews or newspaper stories, poems, comic books, diary entries and more besides.

Any of these can be adapted for use in other subjects. For example:

- Write a series of diary entries imagining how Euclid might have felt while trying to develop his version of geometry.

- Use your knowledge as well as the information from the lesson to write an imaginary interview with Christopher Columbus.

- Write a short story which illustrates some of the benefits and drawbacks tourism brings.

Learning Reviews

30 A learning review involves you and your pupils stopping, taking stock and examining what has been learnt, how it has been learnt and how everything might be improved over the course of the next few lessons.

It can take the form of a whole-class discussion, a piece of independent writing or a series of group discussions, the results of which are then passed to the teacher.

You might like to provide your pupils with some questions they can use to structure their reviews as well as a specific goal they are aiming for as part of the process (for example: To set one target through which to improve my learning in lessons).

Review Writing

31 Reviews abound in our society – book reviews, film reviews, theatre reviews. And now, with the changes wrought by the internet, reviews are even more popular. Just hop onto Amazon or Ebay if you don't believe me!

One thing that unites all reviews is the fact that they involve a judgement (even if the quality of these judgements can vary wildly).

Put this to use in your classroom by having your pupils write reviews. Here are just some of the things they could review:

- Arguments

- Ideas

- Sources

- Characters

- Books, plays, poems and articles

Teacher Quizzes

32 Quizzes are a great way to test the knowledge of your students. You can also use them to provoke thinking and as a means by which to encourage reflection on present understanding (as well as identification of which areas need more work). Here are three ways you can use quizzes:

- At the start of lessons to revisit and recap previous learning.

- At the end of lessons to encourage reflection on and reinforcement of the learning done through the course of the lesson.

- Mid-way through a lesson to help pupils get an immediate sense of the progress they are making.

Student Quizzes

33 As an alternative to teacher quizzes, why not have your students come up with their own ones? Here are three approaches you might like to try:

- Divide the class into groups of five. Each group comes up with five questions. Groups take it in turns to test their peers (and you might like to keep a running total so as to see who wins).

- Divide the class into pairs. Each pair develops ten questions. Pairs then team up and take it in turns to quiz each other.

- Split the class in two. Each half comes up with ten questions which they then use to quiz the other half. The group who answer the most correctly are the winners. (Do point at that teams must be able to give full and correct answers to their own questions!).

Exam Questions

34 Possibly the best way to prepare students for exams is to have them practise exam questions during your lessons. This helps them to get a sense of what examiners are looking for as well as the techniques which they need to hone in order to be successful when sitting the final test.

You can develop this activity by coupling it with a peer-assessment exercise in which pupils mark each other's work using the relevant mark scheme. This helps students to cultivate a clearer understanding of precisely what it is they need to do in their exams in order to be successful.

Compare and Contrast

35 Compare and contrast activities help students to critically analyse different ideas or pieces of information. Juxtaposing two separate items allows us to distinguish each individual item more clearly, as if the light of one illuminates certain aspects of the other which, otherwise, would be hard to see.

Here are some examples of compare and contrast activities:

- Compare and contrast the use of persuasive language in a newspaper report and in a speech.

- Compare and contrast the two different solutions people are putting forward.

- Compare and contrast Hume's arguments about morality with those of Saint Augustine.

Flow-Charts

36 Flow charts help students visualise processes or changes over time. As such, they offer an alternative route into certain types of knowledge. To illustrate this point, consider the difference between a written description of doing the laundry and a flow-chart visualising the process.

Here are three examples of flow-chart based activities:

- Create a flow-chart showing how Lennie's character changes over the course of the book.

- Create a flow-chart showing how the water cycle works.

- Create a flow-chart showing how it can be argued that the Treaty of Versailles led to World War Two.

Spider Diagram

37 Spider diagrams are another way in which students can visualise information. They are particularly good to use at the start of a lesson, at the start of a unit of work, or prior to the completion of a longer piece of writing (as they allow pupils to get all their ideas down on paper before beginning).

You can ask students to produces spider diagrams individually, in pairs or in groups.

You could even work together to create a spider diagram as a whole class.

Glossaries

38 Near the beginning of a unit of work, ask your students to work in pairs to create a glossary for the topic. Provide them with research materials such as textbooks, dictionaries and hand-outs which they can use to help them in this process.

Towards the end of the activity, ask pairs to share their work so that they can check they have the right definitions and to see if they have missed out any important words.

You can ask pupils to work from scratch or you can provide a list of words for which students need to find definitions.

To raise the level of challenge, ask pupils to come up with examples to illustrate the definitions they give.

Comprehension

39 Comprehension activities are all tasks in which you ask students to demonstrate they have processed and understood some specific information. While many tasks involve an element of comprehension, you can also have stand-alone comprehension activities. Here are three examples:

- A piece of text accompanied by a series of questions about the text.

- Questions which require students to explain, outline and describe.

- Tasks in which students have to produce a summary, a précis, or in which they have to pull out the key messages from a piece of text.

Keyword Practice

40 Practising using keywords is important because it helps students to develop their understanding of the language which underpins the subject they are studying. In addition, it gives them an opportunity to reinforce and improve their memories of those keywords.

Here are three activities you can use:

- Present a list of keywords and a discussion topic. Ask pupils to discuss the topic in pairs, using at least one of the keywords every time they speak.

- Set a written task accompanied by a range of keywords. Indicate the minimum number of keywords which students must include in their writing.

- Chant new keywords as a whole class or develop short lyrics or rhyming couplets which include the keywords.

Guides, Leaflets and Posters

41 All three of these activities are good when there is a lot of new information you would like students to synthesise. In each case, pupils need to assimilate the learning and then assess how they can convey their new knowledge and understanding within the framework (or genre) of a guide, leaflet or poster.

As ever, the best chance of success and good progress can be ensured by providing clear success criteria outlining what students will need to include in order to produce the best work possible.

The creation of guides, leaflets or posters can be nicely followed up by peer-assessment in which pupils analyse each other's work and give feedback on whether or not it has met the success criteria.

Continuum

42 Display a double-ended arrow on the board. At one end there should be the words, 'strongly agree' and at the other end it should read, 'strongly disagree.'

Present pupils with a statement connected to the topic and ask them to come to the front of the room and position themselves on the continuum at the point which reflects their opinion on the matter.

Next, lead a discussion in which you encourage pupils in different positions to justify their opinions and to engage in debate with their peers.

An alternative approach sees students writing out the reasons behind their opinions first and then bringing these up to the front with them. They can then refer to these during the course of the discussion.

Student Teachers

43 Appoint a group of five students whose job it is to research a particular topic while you are teaching the rest of the class about something else. This activity often works well if you select particularly able pupils for the role.

After sufficient time has passed, divide the class into five groups and assign each group one of the five students. These pupils should now teach their group about the topic they have been researching.

Alternatively, divide the class into six groups and assign a different topic to each group. They should research this and then teach what they have found out to the rest of the class (with each group coming up to the front in turn).

Questions and Answers

44 Divide the class in two. Give one half of the class a set of questions. Ensure there is one per student and that each one is printed on a single sheet of paper. Give the other half of the class the corresponding set of answers.

Stand back and ask students to match themselves up! Lots of discussion, analysis and questioning should ensue...

Research

45 You can use research tasks in almost any lesson. Generally, they involve pupils working individually, in pairs or in groups to research a topic specified by the teacher. In addition, the teacher will often present a research question designed to guide students in their task.

A couple of variations are as follows.

First, present pupils with the topic of study and then invite them to formulate their own research questions. Provide a range of research materials they can use (or give them access to computers) before leaving them to work independently.

Second, scaffold the research pupils are doing by providing a research question followed by a series of sub-questions. Students can use the sub-questions to guide themselves through the course of the activity.

Think-Pair-Share

46 This is a lovely activity you can slip into your lesson at the drop of a hat. Simply pose a question to the class, ask students to think about it (perhaps giving them 60 seconds silent thinking time), then ask them to discuss their thoughts with their partner before you go on to lead a discussion in which many pupils have the opportunity to share their thoughts with the class as a whole.

Circle Time

47 Arrange the room so that there is a circle of chairs. Invite students to sit in the chairs. Introduce a discussion topic. This could be in the form of a question, a statement or a general topic area which can then be freely explored.

Ask pupils to begin by talking to their partner about their first thoughts on the matter in hand. From this point, build up a discussion by asking various students to share their ideas, comment on other people's ideas and ask questions of the group.

Many teachers like to have an item which the person who is speaking must hold. This is akin to the conch which features in The Lord of the Flies. The advantage of this approach is that it regulates speaking and listening in the group and provides a clear focal point for all students.

Mantle of the Expert

48 This is an innovative, drama-based approach to pedagogy developed by Dorothy Heathcote in the United Kingdom. You can discover more by visiting www.mantleoftheexpert.com. The website is full of useful information and practical ideas presented with great clarity and care. So no need for me to go over everything here as well!

Philosophy for Children

49 As with Mantle of the Expert, so with Philosophy for Children. A great website exists, (http://www.sapere.org.uk/) giving detailed information about this democratic, philosophical approach to pedagogy, much-used and much-admired around the globe.

Competitions

50 And so we come to the end of our energetic run down of 50 quick and easy lesson activities by turning to competitions. Not all teachers like to use them but many students do respond positively to them; some pupils more positively than to anything else!

You can turn almost any activity into a competition (although I would advise you to ration your use of them). With that said, here are two specific competition activities for you to try out:

- Present a set of ten questions, divide the class into groups and indicate the first group to find all ten correct answers will be the winners.

- Divide the class into pairs. Ask each pair to write down the letters A-Z. Introduce the topic and explain that the first team to get a word or phrase connected to the topic for each letter of the alphabet will be the winners.

A Brief Request

If you have found this book useful I would be delighted if you could leave a review on Amazon to let others know.

If you have any thoughts or comments, or if you have an idea for a new book in the series you would like me to write, please don't hesitate to get in touch at mike@mikegershon.com.

Finally, don't forget that you can download all my teaching and learning resources for **FREE** at www.mikegershon.com.

CPSIA information can be obtained
at www.ICGtesting.com
Printed in the USA
LVOW04s1806030216
473528LV00032B/943/P